BASKETBALL HALL OF FAMERS

LARRY BIRD

Mark Beyer

the rosen publishing group's
rosen
central

For Dylan, who drives hard to the hoop

Published in 2002 by The Rosen Publishing Group, Inc.
29 East 21st Street, New York, NY 10010

Library of Congress Cataloging-in-Publication Data

Beyer, Mark (Mark T.)
Larry Bird / by Mark Beyer.
p. cm. — (Basketball Hall of Famers)
Includes bibliographical references and index.
ISBN 0-8239-3484-5 (lib. bdg.)
1. Bird, Larry, 1956-—Juvenile literature. 2. Basketball
players—United States—Biography—Juvenile literature.
3. Basketball coaches—United States—Biography—Juvenile
literature. [1. Bird, Larry, 1956- 2. Basketball players.]
I. Title. II. Series.
GV884.B57 B49 2001
796.323'092—dc21

2001004382

Manufactured in the United States of America

contents

The ABCs of a Champion

The story is a common one: A young boy struggles to escape from the inner city or a placid Midwest farm to become a famous athlete. And then there is the story of Larry Bird. He too worked as hard as any professional athlete, and he came from a Midwest farming community. However, that is where the common story ends. The truth is that Larry Bird wasn't battling to get out of his home state of Indiana at all. In fact, he almost passed up an opportunity that no young man with basketball talent would have dreamt of: He nearly didn't attend college at all. That decision might have ruined any chance that he had to play in the National Basketball Association (NBA).

Larry Bird, who was chosen Most Valuable Player three times by the NBA, is one of the most successful basketball players of all time.

Bird liked living in his small Indiana town. He also liked working for the town, which paid him more money than either of his parents had ever earned. And although he didn't know it yet, he wanted much more from life than just playing basketball with his brothers and friends. The answers he found tell the story of how Bird became a basketball legend.

Midwestern Roots

Larry Bird, the fourth child in a family of six children, was born December 7, 1956, in Bedford, Indiana. His brothers, Michael and Mark, and sister, Linda, were his elder siblings, and Jeff and Eddie were born a few years after him. Their parents, Georgia and Claude "Joey" Bird, raised the children in West Baden until Larry was twelve years old. It was the same small town where he would later star on the basketball team.

Larry was a large infant; at birth, he was more than twenty inches long and weighed almost twelve pounds. His height was not

Larry Bird came from humble beginnings and lived much of his childhood in this modest home in the farming town of West Baden, Indiana.

surprising; his brothers were already taller than normal for their ages. Georgia Bird was nearly six feet tall herself. The difference for Larry was that his height would be appreciated in a state that thrived on its love of basketball.

Even as a child, Larry had some obstacles to overcome. One of them resulted from an unstable family life. Larry's father, Joey Bird, was a heavy drinker who drifted from one job to the next. He was a construction worker, but he had also earned wages at a piano and organ manufacturing company, and at a shoe factory. Larry's father was an abusive person when he drank alcohol. Neighbors and friends could hear arguments between Georgia and Joey Bird on many evenings. Sometimes, they noticed bruises around Georgia's eyes after these yelling matches.

The Bird family believed that many of Joey Bird's troubles stemmed from the time he served in the military. In 1949, he joined the army, with an idea of making a career of the military. Next, he was sent to Korea and fought in the war there. Two years later he came home a changed man. On September 20, 1951, he married Georgia Kerns. For the rest of his life, Joey Bird would wake up with nightmares of watching his friends die in the Korean War. He had also killed his share of men, and these horrible experiences plagued him. Joey Bird was trying to dull his senses and memories of war by drinking, but his abusive personality was hurting his family.

The Bird children lived with their father's abuse as best they could. One way for the kids to escape was to play basketball. Larry was only eight years old when he followed his older brothers to the playground to play. He sometimes had to sit and watch while Michael and Mark played in pickup games. When Larry wanted to join and his brothers refused, he would go home and tell his dad. Joey Bird made sure Michael and Mark allowed Larry to join their games. Soon, Larry's older brothers wanted him to play on their side when he began showing a natural talent for the game.

Practice Makes Perfect

Some of Larry's habits on the basketball court came from those early days of playing. His brothers and their friends were older and bigger than he was, and sometimes they played rough. He learned to take the punishment, but he also learned how to dish it out. He fought for every loose ball, and he struggled to get inside and closer to the hoop. He learned to rebound "playground style," by pounding his body against the opposition. Larry was learning how to play hard-nosed basketball.

Larry did not compete in organized games until much later. In fact, it took an episode in his playground playing days for him to prove to himself how much he loved basketball. One day he was visiting relatives in Hobart, Indiana. As he walked past a playground, some kids asked him if he wanted to play. Larry remembers that day clearly, and he wrote about it in his autobiography, *Drive*. "I took my first shot in the game and it went in. I took my second shot and that went in, too . . . The kids on my team started slapping me on the back and telling me what a great player I was."

When Larry confessed to the kids that he didn't play on any team back home, they were amazed. They asked him to come back the next week to play again. "That was it," Larry wrote. "I was hooked on basketball. I went home and started practicing every morning. I found that the more I did something, the better I got at it."

Bird's early days on the court prepared him for the heavy contact and rough playing style of professional basketball.

Learning the Game

Larry credits his early coach Jim Jones with teaching him the fundamentals of basketball. Jones coached Larry during his early days before high school. "He taught me every basic move there is," Larry remembered. Once he learned those fundamentals—dribbling, shooting, passing, rebounding—Larry used his mind to become a better player. He discovered that his body and his shooting touch were often not good enough against his bigger brothers. Larry began teaching himself other moves, different shots, and false maneuvers to outwit his opponents. His older brother, Mike, remembered those times in Mark Shaw's book, *Larry Legend*: "I think that Larry just reached the point where he didn't want to be beaten anymore. So, he began finding ways to beat you. He was always thinking about the game; figuring strategy."

Strategy and out-thinking an opponent can take a basketball player only so far, however. A good player has to shoot and pass well to make it onto a team. Bird practiced his shooting skills constantly. He often practiced alone. "When I'm out there by myself," he recalled in *Larry Legend* of his early basketball days, "what I'm doing is practicing my rhythm. You can play three-on-three for an hour and a half and you'll possibly take one hundred shots. I can go out myself in the same time and take one-thousand [shots] . . . anywhere I want."

For Larry, practicing basketball came easy. As a boy and as a young man, he had no interests other than sports, especially since his family had limited funds for the children to do much else. Simply put, the Bird family was poor. "Mom and dad always worked so hard," Larry recalled in *Drive*, "but our family was too big for our means. Dad was lucky if he made $120 a week and mom $100. We were always in the hole for money. All of us kids helped with our paper routes and odd jobs, but it still wasn't enough."

He never seemed to miss the advantages that having money brought, such as trips to the local movie theater. He had only basketball for entertainment. Larry used his time wisely, though. What he learned alone, and on the court, would soon serve him very well.

High School Stardom

When Larry Bird entered his senior year at Springs Valley High School in September 1974, Coach Gary Holland knew he had someone special on the Blackhawks. College scouts from around the country waited to see how much better Bird would get. The year before, as a junior, Bird was flawless. He hustled on defense, passed like a pro, and scored like an all-star. Many top basketball colleges wanted him to play for their teams.

Yet all of this might not have happened at all. Bird's temper almost ruined his chances to play in high school. As an eighth-grader, Larry played basketball in French Lick, Indiana. The townspeople called it "biddy ball," and Larry played on the team that was sponsored by a local business. As good a player as he was, his temper was more prominent than his play. He often yelled at players and screamed at referees, racking up plenty of technical fouls. His coach, Butch Emmons, had to bench him twice during that eighth-grade season. After the second incident, he didn't show for the next practice. Coach Emmons kicked him off the team.

High school coach Gary Holland knew of Bird's temper. He also knew he had a potentially great player. He needed to somehow get through to Bird that his temper was going to hurt his game. Holland appealed to Georgia Bird as well as to her son. Somehow, Bird heard what was being said to him. He began to concentrate on his game and ways to control his temper.

On the Team

Bird made the junior varsity team and won a trophy for the most free throws made during his freshman year. By his sophomore year, he was six feet one and 131 pounds. His brother Mark also played for the Springs Valley team and led them in scoring. Now Bird was set to get some of that newsprint that his brother had earned.

A roadblock to early glory appeared quickly when a teammate fell on Bird's ankle, breaking it. He sat on the floor and immediately knew his season was over.

Bird's injury did not keep him from practicing, however. He stood on his crutches and shot baskets every day. A friend rebounded his shots. Bird practiced for hours each day, preparing for his junior year on the basketball court. What he missed was going to the games. He refused to sit on the bench and watch his team play. For Bird, not being able to play was agony. He later said in his autobiography *Drive*, "It just made me too nervous to sit and watch. If I couldn't play, I didn't want to be there."

Bird fought to return to the team before the end of his sophomore season. He also showed that he could play with pain. He proved to his high school coaches that he was ready for the Springs Valley varsity team. At the end of the year, the high school tournament team included the lanky sophomore. In one such varsity game, Bird was

Bird poses here with a basketball during his first year with the Boston Celtics. The team would later remember him as one of its most accomplished players in history.

put in during the second half. "The first time I got the ball, I launched it from about twenty feet and it went in," he remembered. "The crowd went absolutely crazy while I'm passing everywhere, rebounding, sinking all my shots."

Bird stayed in the game and was fouled with only a minute left to play. Springs Valley was down by one point. If he made the two free throws, the team would win the game. "I go to the free throw line and I try to pretend it's 6:00 AM in the gym back home . . . and these [shots] are just two of the five hundred free throws that I shoot every morning. Swish! Both shots are good and we win the game by one point. Pandemonium," he recounted in *Drive*. "Larry Legend," as he would be called as a Celtic in the 1980s, had arrived at stardom.

Young Fame

Bird's name was all over the local newspapers the following day. "I couldn't believe that it was my name in all the stories, and that something that I loved to do—and could do well—could make so many people happy," he said in *Larry Legend*.

That winning day at the free throw line was just the beginning. Over the summer, Bird grew two additional inches and now stood six feet three inches tall. When he began his junior season, he played point guard and loved the position. As a big man, he would normally have played in the forward position. His coaches, however, saw a much more talented player than a "catch and shoot" type. Bird had learned how to pass the ball very well. Most of the time he didn't care who scored for the team as long as they won.

"Once I realized I could pass the ball, my game changed completely," he recalled in *Larry Legend*. "If other guys score, you see the gleam in their eyes. Besides, passing is more of an art than scoring."

The Springs Valley Blackhawks posted a season record of 19 wins and just 3 losses. Bird was a good player—not yet great, but good. As the second leading scorer on the team, he would be a better team player during his senior year. His coaches also thought that he might get a scholarship to one of the nearby junior colleges.

Bird Watching

Three more inches were added to Bird's height over the summer between his junior and senior years. He had also begun using weights to supplement his workout. As a result, he walked onto the basketball court as a high school senior, standing at six feet seven inches tall and ready to battle the best players that Indiana high school basketball could throw at him. Best of all, his coaches noticed, Bird had not lost any of his ball-handling skills. If anything, they had gotten better.

Bird's height and strength made him a natural choice to play in the center position. When Coach Holland, who had taken over as the new Springs Valley High School varsity coach, saw Bird play, he knew immediately that the senior had great potential. Bird did not disappoint him or the Springs Valley Blackhawks. He began the season by shooting confidently and rebounding shots like a man on a mission.

By his senior year, several state colleges and even some national scouts had heard about Bird—a buzz that grew with each passing game. The kid from the small Indiana town was getting a great deal of recognition. Players, coaches, and fans from all over Indiana began "Bird watching"—coming out to see the seventeen-year-old hardwood court phenomenon sink the ball into the hoop.

They were looking to avenge a loss from the year before, but Bird never gave them a chance. He scored more than 30 points for the Blackhawks, and Springs Valley High School won the game.

Once, over a December weekend, Bird scored a combined 97 points in only two games. On Friday night, he reached 42 points in a contest against West Washington High School. The following day, in a game against Corydon High School, Bird scored another 55 points. He also grabbed a phenomenal 24 rebounds!

"Bird watching" was the new state pastime for many basketball fans. For others, however, Bird represented something else; he was now a star destined to be on the roster of a large college or university team. During one high school game, eight college coaches turned out to see him play. All were impressed. The "General" himself, Bobby Knight, coach of the Indiana "Hurrying" Hoosiers, came to watch Bird play in several games. "He's a good scorer," Knight told reporters, "and he has all the required offensive skills, and as good a pair of hands as I've seen all year."

Glory Missed Again

The Springs Valley Blackhawks won their conference championship with ease. They passed through the sectional games as well. The state regional finals, however, found the Blackhawks outgunned by a larger school with a stronger team. Bedord High School sent them to the showers. Much to the disappointment of fans, who turned out in the hundreds to watch

Going from the quiet of the country to the bustling action of Indiana University in the city of Bloomington proved a little much for Bird.

him score, Bird scored only 15 points in his final high school basketball game.

Coming from a small-town school hurt Bird's chances to capture the biggest and best of Indiana's high school basketball honors. He was picked for several all-state teams, but was not even on the ballet for Mr. Basketball. These awards did not hurt his chances for a spot on a college team; even without them, the scouts knew talent when they saw it. Although, for Bird, part of the glory was being recognized by his home state of Indiana, he would have to find glory another way.

With all of his fame and status, Bird still felt like a country boy. And even though his friends knew he was a star basketball player, he was still the same person who spent his days with them down at the local service station. They played pool together at Shorty's, a nearby hangout. They dated neighborhood girls and sometimes cruised to the drive-in theater.

Leaving town was not one of the things he was looking forward to doing. His roots were firmly based in both French Lick and West Baden, Indiana. He felt at home there, naturally, and his shyness would be that much more of an obstacle if he was to attend a large university.

Bird knew he could play with the likes of Big Ten Conference basketball players. To him, this was an unquestionable challenge that he wanted to meet. His true problem was leaving

Indiana. All he really wanted to do was to earn enough money so that he could help his family. He wanted to earn enough money so that his mother would no longer have to work.

College Choices

Joey and Georgia Bird were not about to let their son pass up a chance to get an education, especially if he was sponsored with an athletic scholarship. On one hand, Joey Bird wanted his son to attend Indiana State University (ISU) in Terre Haute because he figured the small state school was more to his son's liking than a larger college. Georgia, on the other hand, liked the prospects of Indiana University. She thought it would be a better arena for her son to show off his athletic gifts so that he could ultimately fulfill his dream: to play as a professional in the NBA.

Bird himself was interested in several schools, including Purdue University, Indiana University, and Indiana State University, but there were others that were calling for the athletic star, too. A funny story surrounds his decision not to attend Louisville College. Louisville coach Denny Crum bet Bird in a game of H-O-R-S-E that if Bird lost, he would come play at Louisville. If the coach lost, Crum would leave French Lick and never bother Bird again. After he creamed the coach in only five shots, Bird sent him packing.

In the end, Bird decided on Indiana University and Bobby Knight's Hoosier team. He would stay in Indiana and play on a nationally known team for a well-known coach. The small-town boy was about to see the outside world.

College All-Star

L ike nearly everything else in his life, Larry Bird's entrance into college in 1974 began on a rocky road. He would be only one of Indiana University's more than 30,000 students in a huge city. Because he was a poor kid from a small town, the environment overwhelmed him. After only twenty-four days, Bird left Bloomington, Indiana, for good.

In *Drive*, Bird points to two key factors that contributed to his decision to leave the school. "I wasn't ready for a school the size of Indiana University. Thirty-three thousand students was not my idea of a school—it was more like a whole country for me . . . [And] I had no money. I mean *no* money. I arrived there with $75. All I had was five or six pairs of jeans, a couple of pairs of slacks, a few shirts, some T-shirts, and my tennis shoes. I didn't even have a sport coat or a pair of dress shoes."

He found himself terribly out of place and at the mercy of his roommate, of whom he asked to borrow clothing, and then money. Finally, he saw the writing on the wall. "I said to myself, 'How can I keep wearing Jim Wisman's clothes and accepting his money?'" The answer was that he could not. He left the school shortly afterward.

Some mystery surrounds the truth behind Bird's leaving IU. Over the years, there were reports that perhaps Bird and Coach Knight did not get along well. Bird, however, never shared that opinion. "Coach Knight had nothing to do with it. Everything was just too big, even the [school's] halls. I couldn't even hear the teachers. I got lost in the shuffle. I like to be around small groups of people and there were so many times [when] I didn't know where I was going." Still, these stories of their mismatch were reported for many years. Bird later explained, "I love Bobby Knight. I think he's the best coach in the nation. He loved my game."

But Bird left IU before basketball practice had even started and didn't explain his departure to Coach Knight. In a matter of weeks, he was back home in French Lick. It was then that his mother suggested he enroll at Northwood Institute, a local junior college much closer to home. He planned to play basketball for the college but found instead that he was lucky for never having suited up.

A Red Shirt Year

After a few practices with the Northwood team, Bird discovered a pressing problem: If he played basketball on the junior college team, he would have to wait two years before he could transfer to another university. He quickly dropped out and changed his plans. He would sit out his freshman year (called a "red shirt") so that he could enroll at a university the following fall and still have four years of NBA eligibility.

For the time being, Bird was happy just being closer to home. He got a job with the French Lick Department of Sanitation. It was ironic— one the country's most talented basketball players driving a garbage truck, painting park benches and fire hydrants, and cleaning sewers. While many people said that Bird had wasted a year of his life and had ruined his chances for a great athletic career, he thought differently. "I was making about $140 to $150 a week, and I was happy. I was able to save some money and I bought my first car, a 1964 Chevy."

Bird didn't care about the opinions of others. He was playing basketball with his friends on a local Amateur Athletic Union team. And he also practiced during the rest of his free time. The team for which he played beat the Indiana All-Stars (a team made up of Indiana's best high school players). Bird scored 39 points that night and wowed the crowd. Some locals thought that he had failed Indiana University. Others thought that he should be playing for Northwood Institute. People who knew him—and many who didn't—tried to convince him that he belonged in a college that could help him make it to the professional league. Bill Hodges, an assistant coach for Indiana State University (ISU), voiced that very same opinion.

Back in the Game

Everyone in the French Lick–West Baden area had an opinion about their favorite son. But Bird just wanted to play basketball. He'd had a rough experience in Bloomington, trying to establish himself within its huge university, and now he wanted to rest his mind without thinking at all about college.

Still, there were coaches from different parts of the Midwest and across the country who wouldn't let him alone. They called so often that Georgia Bird began to worry, but Larry didn't let it affect him much.

Bill Hodges came down from Terre Haute to watch Bird play an exhibition game. He was so impressed that he continued to make the ninety-minute trip just to see him. Larry found that

Hodges was different from the other scouts and coaches. Hodges was from Indiana and a farmer to boot, so he knew about Bird's life.

Hodges finally got his chance to talk with Bird when the player agreed to meet with the coach and his assistant, Stan Evans. Although Georgia Bird was not pleased with the persistence, she trusted her son's judgment. Once Bird and Hodges spoke, he found that he liked the coach very much. Bird understood what he needed to do to become a professional basketball player. Bird agreed to come up to Terre Haute and meet with Bob King, the head coach for Indiana State.

Bird, his brother Mark, and another Springs Valley player, Kevin Carnes, drove to the ISU campus. Together, with two other players from ISU, they made up a team. They played the ISU starters and clobbered them. "No contest," Bird remembered. "We drilled them. Hodges couldn't believe it." The coach was amazed, but maybe more so because the trio from French Lick played in jeans and sneakers.

By the middle of the summer of 1975, Bird had moved to Terre Haute. He enrolled at ISU and prepared to play basketball. There was just one problem: College rules forced Bird to sit out for one year. Coach King could not use him as a Sycamore during those games. He could, however, use Bird as his practice starter. The opportunity was there to allow the latent basketball star to hit the courts. The Larry Show was about to begin.

Blue Against White

It was obvious to Coach King that Bird was his best player. Bird and the white team took apart the starting blue team in nearly every practice. It was always the same scenario: Bird was constantly passing, shooting, posting up, and rebounding. The blue team began to lose confidence. Coach King realized that if he didn't use him to help them get better, his Sycamore team would be losers during the entire season.

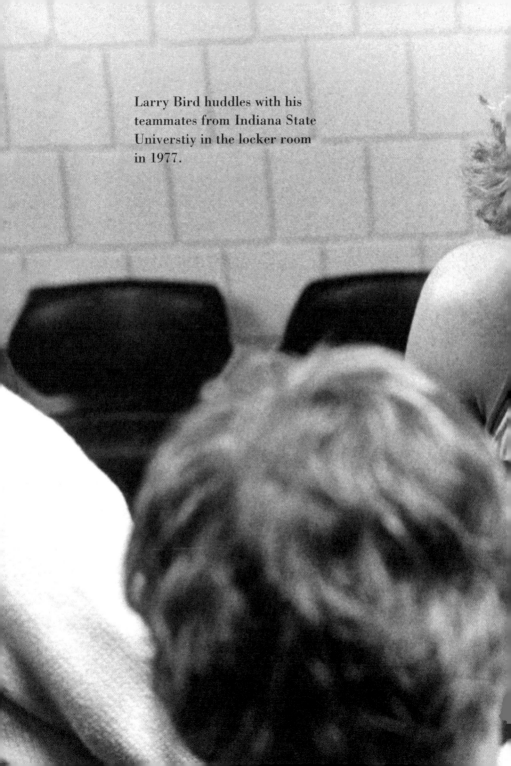

Larry Bird huddles with his teammates from Indiana State Universtiy in the locker room in 1977.

When King first approached Bird about not playing so hard during the scrimmages, Bird's temper nearly got the better of him. He told King that he was going to quit. He wanted to know how he was supposed to play, if not to his own skill level. Practice and scrimmage games were his only method to maintain his skills. "Look, Larry," King recalled telling him, "I can't get anything done with these other guys. You make them look like idiots." This argument made sense, but Bird still practiced as hard as ever. During scrimmages, though, he learned to allow the starters to grow as a team.

Growing Too Quickly

Although Bird spent nearly all of his time playing basketball, he still had time to fall in love. He met Janet Condra at ISU, and on November 8, 1975, the two were married. He and Janet were often at odds with each other, however, because she didn't understand why her new husband's life was completely devoted to basketball.

Larry wrote of their relationship in *Drive*, "I knew right away it wasn't going to work. I tried to make it work, but there was just no way." The young couple had been too young and immature to marry. They filed for divorce around the same time that Janet became pregnant. At the time, Larry had already begun another relationship with Dinah Mattingly. And although he rarely saw Janet and their daughter, Corrie, Bird reached out to her later, promising to provide her support, guidance, and love.

Meanwhile, Larry and Dinah became closer than ever. She loved basketball, and Larry appreciated the fact that they could laugh together and have a good time while he did what he did best. They fell in love. "I realized she was the one," Bird recalled. "She was beautiful, athletic, understanding, funny, and [above all she was] my friend." The two eventually got married and have been together ever since.

Playing for the Sycamores

Bird played his first college basketball game as a sophomore. In preseason play, the Sycamores played the Brazilian national team. Larry scored 31 points to lead ISU to victory. Everyone watching that game saw something special in Bird. They knew they had a winner and hoped the Sycamores would go far in National Collegiate Athletic Association (NCAA) play.

ISU went to the National Invitational Tournament (NIT) in the spring of 1976. In the semifinals, the Sycamores played against the Houston Cougars. Otis Birdsong, another future NBA star, led the Cougars. In a game the press dubbed "The Battle of the Birds," Bird scored 44 points, while Birdsong scored only 30. But the Cougars won the game 83–82, when Bird's last shot went off the rim.

That first season was educational for Bird, who learned about how to further control his temper. Still, he talked trash to opponents—something he would become famous for on the Celtics—and played hard-nosed basketball.

Bird goes for a jump shot during a game against Bradley University in 1978.

Waiting to Win

Bird scored great numbers during his first year as a college player. He ranked third in the nation with an average of 32.4 points per game and had an NCAA ranking of seventh in rebounds. With numbers like these, many thought he would leave college early and enter the pros, but he was committed to ISU.

"Money isn't everything," Georgia Bird told reporters, who recounted her wishes for her son in *Larry Legend*. "Larry has two years in school and I'd like to see him stay."

The rumors were true—money was available—and many NBA teams were waiting for Bird's decision. They needed a player like him to help the struggling league regain popularity, but Bird disappointed those early bidders. Despite earning third-team all-American honors, he was staying put. He knew he had a lot to learn.

Bird's junior year at ISU saw the Sycamores stack fifteen wins. The team faltered down the stretch and finished with a season record of 19–7. During the Missouri Valley

Conference Tournament, however, Bird hurt his back. Actually, he was injured not on the court but when a teammate jumped on his back during a team celebration.

Bird received medical treatments before the big game against Creighton. He also took painkillers to help him get through. Even with an ailing back, he still scored 29 points. It just wasn't enough, though. His Sycamores lost by 2 points and failed to get in the NCAA Tournament. The team's strong play and solid season record helped them secure a second invitation to the NIT. They beat Illinois State but lost to New Jersey's Rutgers University. It was yet another bittersweet season because Bird was named all-American, but his team failed to live up to his expectations. He tried to focus instead on the next college season, which would be his last.

More Rumors, a Steal, and a Stunning Season

During the summer before Bird's senior year, there were more rumors insinuating that he

Coach Bill Hodges consoles Bird after the Indiana State University Sycamores lose the championship to Michigan State in March 1979.

would enter the pros, but he was still committed to college. Just in case, Boston Celtics general manager, Red Auerbach, drafted Bird as the sixth player overall in the June 1978 NBA draft. He and the Celtics had given up a choice draft spot for Bird, but they would have to wait an entire season to use the college star. If he became better the following year, the Celtics had pulled off the greatest steal in NBA history.

Although Bird headed back to school, his coach, Bob King, was not on the bench when he and the Sycamores returned to action in the fall of 1978. Over the summer, King suffered a heart attack. When an aneurysm appeared shortly afterward, King gave up his coaching duties to Bill Hodges.

Bird and three other seniors returned, along with a group of players who were ready to help the Sycamores make a run for the NCAA title. The season began well, and the Sycamores won their first three games. In their fourth game against Evansville, a shot at the buzzer and Bird's 40 points helped the Sycamores take the lead with a 4–0 start. Two more wins were racked up in the Florida Hatter Classic Tournament. The Sycamores were ranked second in the nation midway through the season, just behind Notre Dame University. A few weeks later, when Bird and the Sycamores won their eighteenth game, every college basketball fan knew that something good was in the air.

The game against archrival Illinois State showed what Bird was made of. The Redbirds put three players on the star, trying to box him in during the entire game. As a result, he scored his lowest total ever, 4 points, but the Sycamores bounced Illinois State 91–72. The following Monday, the NCAA rankings put the Indiana State Sycamores in the nation's number one spot.

The win against Illinois State decided the Missouri Valley Conference Championship. It also put the Sycamores into the number one spot for the NCAA Tournament, the team's first. The Sycamores, now crowned the Magnificent Seven, wanted to show the other teams—and the nation—that a small-town school could win.

Tournament Thrills

Many basketball know-it-alls thought Bird and the Sycamores would lose the NCAA tournament easily. They also said ISU had not played against more than a few nationally ranked teams all year. Their conclusion was that the school's 27–0 record wasn't much to brag about.

Bird wasn't bragging, though. He came to play. Their first game was against Virginia Tech in Lawrence, Kansas. Bird scored 22 points and the Sycamores won easily, 86–69. Their next challenge would be against Oklahoma in Cincinnati. By now, Bird's play was spooking some of the coaches in the path of the Sycamores' run for national glory. (Reportedly more than 500 suggestions were sent to Oklahoma coach Dave Bliss on how to stop Bird.)

Bird scored 29 points and made 15 rebounds against Oklahoma. In the stands, Boston Celtics general manager, Red Auerbach, and Coach Dave Cowens saw their soon-to-be NBA rookie dazzle the crowd. Even the Oklahoma fans cheered for Bird by the game's end.

Bird makes a jump shot past a defender during a game against Purdue University in 1978.

The Sycamores rolled on into the Elite Eight. They battled the Arkansas Razorbacks and Sidney Moncrief. The game became a war and was tied with only seconds left on the clock. Arkansas had a chance at the last-second shot but traveled with the ball instead, giving the Sycamores a second chance. Bird's teammate, Bob Heaton, hit a rim-bobbling shot that fell through the net. At last, ISU was in the Final Four.

A Magical Time

The 1978 NCAA Final Four teams were ISU, Pennsylvania, DePaul, and Michigan State University (MSU), who had a phenomenal player of its own in Earvin "Magic" Johnson. Bird and Johnson had played together before on a traveling all-star team the previous summer. They got along well and had loved each other's style of playing. Now, if both ISU and MSU made it past their opponents, Johnson and Bird would compete against one another.

The consummate sportsman, Bird helps up Michigan State's Magic Johnson during the NCAA Championship in March 1979.

Michigan State ripped Penn apart in their game, winning by 34 points. The ISU Sycamores dueled against Midwestern powerhouse DePaul. The legendary coach, Ray Meyer, had future NBA star Mark Aguirre heading his team. Bird scored 35 points and the Sycamores won 76–74. The stage was set for the big-time Michigan State versus the small-town ISU Sycamores.

On March 26, 1979, Bird met Johnson on the basketball floor in Salt Lake City, but from the opening tip, the Sycamores looked flat. Because they had worked so hard to get there, they were tired and it showed. The match against DePaul had worn them out both physically and emotionally. Bird emerged looking exhausted, and the Michigan State defense, designed exclusively to stop him, worked effectively.

Bird, the star player who had carried ISU all season, was chased around the court for the entire game. He scored only 19 points, and said afterward, as reported in *Larry Legend*, "We thought we had proved that we could beat every kind of defense, but we had never seen anything like that zone of theirs. I couldn't do anything at all against it. They really did a good job on me."

The Michigan State Spartans won that game and the championship. The Sycamores, however, had nothing to cry about, since their first NCAA tournament showing earned them a runner-up spot. They had also finished the season 33–1. Once they returned to Terre Haute, Bird and his teammates knew they had done something spectacular. Years later, Bird talked about his Sycamore team. "We didn't have much raw talent . . . [but] we proved what you could accomplish when you have guys who really believe in each other, who work together, and who know what it takes to win."

Bird, the individualist and the superstar player, had learned what it took to win a championship—a lesson he would remember while playing for the Boston Celtics.

Celtic Pride

Becoming a Celtic was almost as hard for Bird as fighting through that 33–1 Sycamore season. He had hired sports agent Bob Woolf, a Boston attorney, to handle his contract negotiations. Woolf was known around town and throughout the sports world as a tough negotiator.

Such a beginning did not sit well with Red Auerbach, who was a no-nonsense businessman himself. His first reaction to Bird's hiring Woolf was to leak a story to the Boston papers that his star draft pick expected to be paid $1 million a year for six years, a figure that, in 1979 at least, represented an outrageous amount to pay an unproven talent.

Upon signing a five-year, $3 million contract with the Boston Celtics in 1979, Bird, flanked here by Celtics president Red Auerbach and Coach Bill Fitch, became the richest rookie player in sports history.

Bird was still a kid, and the Celtics management knew about his leaving Indiana University because of its size. They were also concerned about Bird's reactions to Boston, a large metropolitan city. Everyone in the sports business, and basketball in particular, knew that the Celtics were taking a risk.

Nevertheless, negotiations proceeded, with heated arguments flaring up between Woolf and the team. Eventually, the two sides agreed to contract terms. Bird would play for the Celtics and receive $600,000 each year for five years. The $3 million contract was the highest paid for a rookie player of *any* sport. He was only twenty-three years old.

The Celtics were a team with tradition. They won ten consecutive NBA titles, from 1959 to 1968, as well as one in 1976, and were one of the founding teams of the league. Now, though, the team was on the skids. The year before the Celtics had gone 32–50 for the season. Something, or someone, was needed, and Auerbach believed it was Bird.

Larry Bird, pictured third from left in the back row, was a rookie player when this team picture was shot for the 1979-1980 Boston Celtics.

Celtic management had also changed coaches. Bill Fitch, an outsider in the Celtic organization, had pulled together a losing Cleveland team and made it into a contender. When Fitch fought with Cleveland management, the Celtics saw an opportunity. They hired Fitch to coach the team and remake them into champions once more.

Bird, who might have thought that Bobby Knight had a reputation for toughness with his players, thought differently when he got his first

taste of Fitch's methods during training camp. "I realized that [Fitch] intended to show me who was boss," Bird said in *Drive*. "When we started the scrimmages, he was doing everything he could to test me. He wanted to aggravate me, and he just couldn't do it. He'd make me guard this player, then another one. He tried to run me until I was ready to drop."

Part of the Celtic pride was the ability to play tough. They got that toughness when they drafted Bird, who dove for loose balls, took an elbow, and then gave an elbow in return. He was pushed around as a rookie but quickly dished it back to show that he was ready for NBA-style basketball. Teammate M. L. Carr, another Celtic newcomer (picked up as a free agent), remembered Bird's impact: "Rookies just don't come in the way Larry [Bird] did. He was making creative passes, joking confidently, and going out and backing up his words with his play."

Bird discovered Celtic pride through his seasoned teammates. Rookies are always tested;

Bird, pictured here taking a breather during a game, was a tough player who really hustled for the ball and proved himself to his teammates very early in his career.

it's the nature of basketball. Coming in as the hot new rookie with a huge contract made Bird a target. Cedric Maxwell was one Celtic veteran who wanted to see what Bird was made of. "Maxwell really wanted a piece of me," Bird remembered. "He had all these veteran-type tricks and we would go at it every day." As Bird remembered those early practices, he was the guy who showed the veterans who could really play and scrap. His hard work showed that he was there to stay.

Rookie Trials and Honors

Like all rookies, Bird started off with up-and-down play. At one point, he told reporters that the ball in the NBA was different from what he'd been used to playing with (the NBA uses a Wilson ball that has narrow seams; the NCAA uses Spalding's brand of wide-seamed ball). He wasn't offering an excuse, just pointing out a problem that he had to overcome. "Once I get used to shooting that ball," Bird told them, "I'll be all right."

As Bird (number 33) watches, his nemesis, Magic Johnson (also number 33) drives past Bird's teammate Carl Nicks to score against ISU.

If his shooting and rebounding skills were a little off in his early games, Bird's passing made up for the uneven play. Ever since high school, he had loved to pass the ball. In the NBA, finding the open man was the key to winning games, and a good passing team found its open players. Bird's passing skills were outstanding.

"That's the way we played at Indiana State," Bird says in *Drive*. "One [player] will want to make a good pass, then the next guy will want to make one. Pretty soon everybody's doing it." Bird passed, Maxwell passed, Carr passed, and the Celtics began to win games.

Magic Johnson left college after winning the NCAA Championship with Michigan State. He was chosen by the Los Angeles Lakers and quickly became their "showtime" player. The first duel between professionals Bird and Johnson happened in December of their rookie years. The Lakers won, but Bird showed Johnson that he was stronger than he was in Salt Lake City, just ten months before.

The Philadelphia 76ers' Julius "Dr. J" Erving tries to make a shot over Bird during a semifinals game in April 1980. The Sixers would prevail over the Celtics.

"Larry thought I was 'Hollywood,'" Johnson told a group of reporters, "egotistical and stuck on myself. I thought he was the country guy who couldn't relate to me and the other guys." In response, Bird said, "He's showtime. I can't play the game smiling and joking. I'm too serious."

The two rookies pounded each other throughout the game. Bird knocked Johnson to the floor late in the game. Johnson rose up and the two players went face-to-face. They had to be pulled apart before fists began to fly.

Playoff Time

The Celtics ended the season with sixty-one wins, the best record in the league. The team came into the playoffs with confidence. They beat the Houston Rockets in the first round, without losing a game. They met the Philadelphia 76ers in the second bout, and Julius "Dr. J" Erving's group trounced them. Bird was crushed at the last defeat, but he came away from the season knowing how to play team basketball with the pros.

Hard-driving coach Bill Fitch of the Boston Celtics saw great talent and potential in Bird during his early seasons with the team.

Like many before him, Celtic coach Bill Fitch saw something special in Bird. "He had an uncanny ability to see the floor," Fitch told reporters. "[His] mind takes an instant picture of the whole court."

Bird's intuition on the court was outstanding, and players, coaches, and announcers alike marveled at the country kid's moves and scoring ability. Throughout his college days and after he had signed with the Celtics, Bird was called "too slow." He was also accused of not being able to jump. But his driven attitude, which forced him to learn how to beat his brothers, was used against the best players in the NBA. Bird won the Rookie of the Year award by a vote of 63–3 over Magic Johnson. He was voted third for MVP, just behind Kareem Abdul-Jabbar and Julius Erving.

Bird enjoyed his newfound fame. His agent, Bob Woolf, saw earning power in him beyond the basketball court, and Bird later signed endorsement deals with Spalding sports equipment and Converse athletic shoes, making him a wealthy young man. He had come a long way from his humble roots in the Midwest.

Still, he was wary of his money. In *Drive*, he wrote about his newfound wealth, "I know a lot of guys [who] go off the first year they come into money and buy everything in sight. Then they find out they didn't have as much money as they thought they did."

Moving Toward the Title

Lucky for Bird, the Celtics' management saw that the team needed more strength and depth around their rookie star. Over the next season, the team grew stronger after adding draft-pick players such as Robert Parish and Kevin McHale.

The added defense was enough to push the Celtics to a second Eastern Division title. They met their rival 76ers in the conference championship but fell behind in the series, three games to one. They rallied to win Game 5, but knew they would have to beat the 76ers on their home turf to have any chance at winning the series. Fitch had his team dress in a different locker room and practice at the opposite end of the court. These psychological tactics worked to free the Celtics from the past experiences of poor play at the 76ers home court. They won the game in a squeaker, 100–98.

Game 7 was played in Boston, and Bird knew the only way to beat the 76ers was to slow down Julius Erving's graceful scoring techniques. "The most important thing I had to do while

Bird silenced many of his critics during the 1981 NBA Finals, when his excellent passing, shooting, and defense helped the Celtics beat the Houston Rockets.

guarding 'Dr. J,'" wrote Bird in *Drive*, "was to get help. When he started going along the baseline, you knew what was on his mind. He wanted to dunk. Once he got a step on you, there was nothing you could do. Any daylight at all and 'Dr. J' would jam it through." The tactic worked, and the Celtics found themselves in the championship.

The 1981 NBA Finals saw Bird showing why he had been voted Rookie of the Year in 1980. His passes were crisp and on target, his shots found the bottom of the net, and his defense stymied each Rocket he went up against. The once slow-footed, small-town boy had proved all his critics wrong yet again.

In Game 6, Boston was up by just a few points. Houston had rallied and their momentum was surging. Bird took the ball in the corner for a three-point shot. "It's all in my hands," he recalled thinking at that moment. He let the shot fly. "When the ball went through the net, my heart started pounding." The Celtics won the game and the series, giving Bird the championship that he'd dreamt of for years.

The Fight Continues

Winning an NBA championship title takes diligence, practice, and sometimes a little luck. The vast majority of players who appear in NBA uniforms never play for a championship, much less win one. Karl Malone has played for sixteen years. He has come close, but he has not won a ring. Charles Barkley was a leader on several teams, but retired before he could get his own ring. Michael Jordan, of course, has been lucky, winning six championships.

Bird and the Celtics of the 1980s were in a league with some extremely strong teams. One was the Los Angeles Lakers, led by Johnson and Abdul-Jabbar. The years that the Celtics and Lakers fought against each other for the championship title were some of the most exciting in basketball history. And early in Bird's career, the 76ers and Celtics constantly battled for the top spot in the division. The most exciting part for Bird was that his Celtic team was near a championship for nearly every year of his thirteen-season career.

After the first championship in 1981, Bird wanted to win again the following season. His play was excellent, and he continued proving that he was going to be a force for years to come. But even though the Celtics grew as a team, they won only fifty-six games that season, losing to the 76ers, who won the division with sixty-five wins. Boston moved into the playoffs. They hoped to gain a rematch with the 76ers in the Conference Finals, but Bird and the Celtics never made it out of the starting gate. In the first round, they were swept by the Milwaukee Bucks.

Recalling the year following his first championship, Bird's competitive nature told the whole story. "It was embarrassing. We never got it together that year." He tried to explain his emotions after losing. "Sitting in the locker room after being swept by the [Milwaukee] Bucks was the worst feeling I've ever had [while] playing basketball. I had known great moments, had won a championship, and had had a lot of good games, but at that moment it seemed like the end of the world."

The Celtics worked harder the following year, but another championship would have to wait. The 76ers had the Celtics' number for the next two years and won the championship in 1983. By 1984, however, Bird and the Celtics had gelled into a powerhouse team. Coach K. C. Jones replaced the hot-tempered Bill Fitch. The team then picked up Dennis Johnson from Phoenix. Johnson's tough defense added dozens of steals for the Celtics. As a new coach, Jones allowed the team to be individuals on the court. His coaching philosophy worked wonders for them.

New players and a new coach helped the Celtics make the NBA Finals in four consecutive years (1984–1987). In 1984 and 1986, Bird won his second and third NBA Championship titles by playing tough basketball. Some people would call it street ball, or back-lot basketball, marked by blocking, pushing, knockdowns, and fighting. Many thought the Celtics played more like a street gang during a rumble. To fans, it was the new style of NBA basketball. To win, you had to be tough, and Bird was never tougher.

The End of an Era

The 1987–1988 season found the Celtics struggling. It seemed that their best years were behind them. The players were much slower, and scores of injuries plagued them. They were also playing against younger, faster players, such as the Detroit Pistons. Michael Jordan and the Chicago Bulls were clawing their way to the top, too. The New York Knicks, Philadelphia 76ers, and Atlanta Hawks were also pushing hard for their own successes.

Bird and the Celtics still played well, but combating all of these teams in the playoffs was becoming a losing battle. Even worse, Bird was carrying the Celtics' scoring load, a signal of defeat for the team. By the time the Celtics lost

During a 1988 tournament in Madrid, Spain, Bird pushes back Antonio Martin of Real Madrid. Bird and company prevailed, 111–96.

against the Pistons in the 1988 playoffs, Bird was exhausted and defeated. A reporter asked him if he was a little tired and he responded, "No, I'm *a lot* tired."

Bird was thirty-one years old and had just finished his ninth NBA season. Including the playoff games in each of those years, he had played more than 800 professional games. The pounding on his body had taken its toll. In fact, Bird had been in pain for years.

Injured and Still on the Court

During Bird's basketball career, he was hit with many injuries. The long list included a broken knuckle, a broken collar bone, torn ligaments in his fingers, a fractured cheekbone, a broken nose, Achilles tendon problems, back problems, and bone spurs on his heels. Still, he played through the pain.

Dell Curry of the Cleveland Cavaliers elbowed Bird in the eye during a game in 1988. The shot broke a bone in his eye socket.

"I knew there was something seriously wrong with my eye. When I looked up, I saw two baskets. One was just a little higher than the other. The pain was intense, and when I looked into the mirror there was an egg-sized bump on my forehead, and my eye was swollen shut," he said in *Drive*. Although forced to wear eye goggles for several games, he still played well.

The Celtics gained yet another new coach, Jimmy Rodgers, in 1988. The team was confident that they could make another run at a championship, but after eight games, their season was shattered. Bird suffered problems in both feet, caused by bone spurs pressing on his tendons. Surgery became necessary, and Bird's season ended. He wrote about his injuries in *Drive*. "That was a year I wish I could have started over. It reminded me of when I was hurt in high school. I could barely manage to watch the games. I missed playing so much it made my stomach hurt."

"What's Wrong, Larry?"

Coach Rodgers had a plan for the 1989–1990 season: Don't focus on Bird. Rodgers thought the veteran player was too old to play as hard as he had before. He was right, but Bird didn't agree. Instead, Rodgers used most of the remaining team, a move that caused the two to argue constantly. Bird took far fewer shots that season than ever before.

At the beginning of the following season, the media began to see that he had lost the motivation that he once had. *Sports Illustrated* asked the question "What's Wrong, Larry?" on one of its covers, but the answer to that question was a complex one. The Celtics had changed since those championship seasons, and different coaches had taken the team in other directions, the results of which made Bird less of a factor in the Celtics' offense. His body was slowing because of age and injury. Without strength, he couldn't jump and shoot like he once did. His game was faltering. At one point, his teammates wondered whether he was helping them at all.

Even towards the end of his career, Larry Bird still had the shooting touch of a champion.

Bird was frustrated. Red Auerbach asked him if he wanted to be a player-coach, but Bird said no. Even though he was fighting back pain, he thought that he could still perform as he once had. He was wrong. He played only sixty games that season.

Last Chance

During the summer break in 1991, Bird had back surgery to correct a nerve that was compressed between two vertebrae. The surgery was successful and helped ease the pain that had hurt Bird for more than five years. At one point in 1985, he was forced to lay on his stomach at the end of the bench during rest periods in an effort to put the least amount of pressure on his back. It was the only way he could play an entire game. That was five years before, and his injury had never healed properly.

Bird's doctor told him that the surgery was successful, but he was still limited as a player who needed every bit of the strength, stamina, and agility of a young athlete. "My back hurt me so bad I could barely move," he recalled in *Bird Watching*, his autobiography. "I became a day-to-day player, something I hated."

By the 1991–1992 season, Bird knew that the end of his career was on the horizon. He had not performed well on the court for awhile, at least not to his own expectations. When a gifted athlete fails to live up to his or her own high standards, he or she may feel that it is better to leave the sport than to suffer embarrassment. And Bird was just that kind of player.

He spoke about retirement privately. His wife, Dinah, urged him to call it quits. She was tired of watching her husband eating his meals while stretched out on the floor. Ever the competitor, Bird decided he would continue. But before the summer's end, he knew that trying to play another season would be pointless. He might injure himself further, a situation that could hurt him permanently. After all, he was only thirty-five years old.

Now retired, Bird pulls
back longtime friend and
sometime adversary Magic
Johnson's LA Lakers
jersey to reveal a Celtics
jersey underneath during a
lighthearted moment.

Farewell to Larry

On August 18, 1992, Bird arranged a press conference in which he announced his retirement to a stunned sports world. In his book *Bird Watching*, he said, "It was one of the happiest days of my life . . . I had been playing through back problems for almost ten years, and I just couldn't take it anymore. The pain was relentless. No matter what I did—whether I was standing up, sitting down, lying down, leaning over—I couldn't escape it . . . It had completely taken over my life." The press and fans had seen this moment coming for several years, but when it happened they realized there would be no more Larry Bird in the NBA. An era had come to an end.

Just before his retirement, he had finished competing in the Olympics. And while in Barcelona, Spain, he found—to his amazement—that he was known around the world, a discovery that pleased the kid from rural Indiana. Ever modest, he didn't think he deserved the attention.

Magic Johnson, an Olympic teammate, had a different opinion of Bird. Over the years, the two competitors had become friends and admired each other's abilities on the court. In his book *My Life*, Johnson saw him as someone who succeeded more by diligence than pure skill. "The amazing thing about Larry [Bird] is that he achieved his success without some of the natural talents that other people take for granted. [Larry Bird] did it the old fashioned way. He worked, and worked, and then worked some more. To most players, basketball is a job. To Larry [Bird], it was his *life*."

Bird Enters the Front Office

For a time, Bird went home to French Lick, Indiana. He rested his back and even began playing golf. After years of fierce competition mixed with a few months of relaxation, however, life in the country was an adjustment. "I'd go to bed at eight o'clock at night and get up at five in the morning," Bird recalled. "[That] wasn't enough to keep my mind working." He needed to be in the action. If he couldn't play, and didn't yet have the burning fire to coach, what could he do to stay in the game he loved?

The Celtics offered him the position of special assistant to the senior executive vice president. It was a job where he could offer his opinions on player drafting, player changes, and overall team strategy. He worked in the Celtics front office for three years before he had a falling-out with the team. The man who hired him, Dave Gavitt, had resigned.

In *Bird Watching*, Bird sees Gavitt's resignation from a different angle. "[The] Celtics owners kind of forced him out, which is really too bad, because Dave Gavitt is a genius. He is very straightforward, which I've always liked in a person."

Afterward, Paul Gaston and Bird's former teammate M. L. Carr ran the team. "[They] would ask my advice about certain personnel moves, then turn around and do

After retiring from playing, Larry Bird worked as a special assistant to the Celtics' senior executive vice president, but left the team after a falling-out with the management.

whatever they wanted. I mean, why ask my opinion if you don't really care what I think?" He quickly knew his days were numbered. "I told our owner that Sherman Douglas was the most valuable guy on our team . . . [and] he traded him a month later." This was 1995, and Bird still hung around for two additional years. "We'd have ten guys in a room trying to make a decision on one player, and it drove me crazy. I'm not saying I had all the answers, but the way they tried to do things, it's a wonder they got anything done," he said in *Bird Watching*.

After more changes in the Celtic organization, Bird left his team forever. He returned to Indiana and the small-town atmosphere. His eyes, however, were fixed on an open coaching position in Indianapolis. Indiana was about to get their hero back in a big way.

Coaching the Pacers

Larry Bird had almost become the Indiana Pacers' head coach in 1993. "[The] timing wasn't right because of my back," he explained in *Bird Watching*. "I was still in such a bad way that I never considered it." He needed additional surgery. This time screws were put into two vertebrae and metal rods held them in place. He was forced to take it easy for more than a year, but the surgery helped. For the most part, he is now able to lead a normal life.

When he came home to Indiana in 1997, he knew that the Pacers' president, Donnie Walsh, was searching for a new coach. "All I heard was that Donnie was just like me, that he would put everything out there, and he

wouldn't pull any punches . . . That's exactly the way it has been. Donnie has never lied to me . . . I knew that two days after I met him. You don't find that very often, especially in this business."

Bird and his wife, Dinah, had always moved together during their early years, especially while he was playing for the Celtics. They had homes in Massachusetts, Indiana, and Florida. During the off-season, they traveled to different cities, but by 1990 their infant children forced them to settle down. Becoming the Pacers' coach was going to be disruptive to his family life, so he signed only a three-year contract. The other reason lay with the team's ability to win a championship, a goal that he believed would take three years. With that, he moved his family to the Indianapolis area.

Stealing from Past Coaches

Bird gives credit for his success as a leader to his former high school coaches, who taught

Head coach Larry Bird calls out orders to his Indiana Pacers during their Eastern Conference Semifinals in May 1998, in which the Indiana Pacers would defeat the New York Knicks, 99–88.

him the fundamentals of basketball and a strong work ethic. He knew that without those traits, he could never have become a good player. He also believed that if you work harder than your opponents do, you increase your chances of winning.

He credits Bill Fitch and K. C. Jones. "Bill was organized, he preached discipline, and he had us in the best shape of our lives." All you have to do is look at how the Celtics won a championship within two years of Bird's arrival to see what Fitch meant to him. From K. C. Jones, he learned control and how to motivate players. Jones was the complete opposite of Fitch in temperament. He worked his players hard, but he did not antagonize them, and Bird took his style of coaching to Indianapolis.

Bird's coaching philosophy worked for the Pacers. The year before, the team won only thirty-nine games, but his new conditioning drills, motivation skills, and play calling helped the team win fifty-eight games during their first year together. They even made it to the Eastern Conference Finals, where they competed against the Chicago Bulls, the team who had won the NBA title the previous two years.

As a coach, he instructed the Pacers to believe in their chances even if most teams in the NBA didn't believe that they could beat Michael Jordan and the Bulls.

"Jordan had become bigger than life," Bird wrote in *Bird Watching*. "Everyone in the league seemed to be afraid of him, or intimidated by him. Somehow the Pacers needed a new mindset, one that would convince them Jordan was human and Chicago was not untouchable."

Even though they went in with the right attitude, the team could not come up with enough strength, shots, or wins to beat the Bulls. They lost the first two games but won Games 3 and 4, proof that they still had a chance. Better yet, one of the Pacers' star players, Reggie Miller, was in top form. "What Reggie had done was huge," Bird recalled.

"He had deflated the whole Michael [Jordan] mystique."

The next game was in Chicago, and the Pacers fell flat. "Their performance in that game broke my heart," Bird wrote. "At that point I began wondering again whether our guys were slipping back into the mentality of 'Nobody beats Michael.'" Bird had played every game thinking that his team would win by 20 points. If he couldn't get his Pacers to believe that, too, he felt he had failed.

His team came back once again, winning Game 6 by the skin of their knees. Before Game 7, Bird gave them a pep talk. It was a change for Bird, who was normally a quiet, unassuming man off the court. But this game was different. "I wanted these guys to understand what it would be like to be a champion," he wrote in *Bird Watching*. "I talked about the respect they would get if they accomplished that. All they had to do was look across the court at Jordan to understand that."

Star player Reggie Miller confers with Coach Larry Bird during Game 2 of the Pacers' effort to win the NBA Finals against the LA Lakers.

With a few minutes of play remaining, a jump ball was called between Pacers' center Rik Smits and Michael Jordan. Smits was much taller than Jordan, and he would most likely get the tip. However, when the teams lined up for the jump ball, Bird noticed something wrong. His players were out of position to get Smits's tip. He would have to tip it backwards, something he was not known to do. Reggie Miller and the Bulls' Scottie Pippin were in the spot where Smits would tip the ball. Worse, Pippin was in front of Miller. Before Bird could call a time-out, the ref threw the ball. The tip was intercepted by Pippin, and the Bulls scored on a three-point shot! Bird was physically sick about his slow reaction to what he'd seen as a problem. His team would have to wait another year.

Hall of Fame Honors

In 1998, Bird was inducted into the Basketball Hall of Fame. His thirteen seasons as a Celtic and three NBA titles made him a natural choice. His famed shooting style, hard-nosed

Despite losing the NBA Finals, Larry Bird was named Coach of the Year for the 1997–1998 season after bringing his Indiana Pacers to a 58–24 record. Here, he jokes during the press conference after being named.

play, and all-around talent worked to give him a unanimous vote.

He asked his former Celtics coach, Bill Fitch, to act as his official presenter, a person who has had a significant impact on that player's life. "[Coach Fitch] said he had no idea I thought that much of him," Bird wrote in *Bird Watching*. "I guess I'm not the best at telling people."

Bird won Coach of the Year honors for the 1997–1998 season. He had pulled the Pacers from a 41–41 win-loss record to a near sixty-game winning season. Now, though, he wanted only one thing: a championship for his players.

Because the Basketball Players' Union and owners were in contract disputes into the start of the new season, games were delayed. The owners had begun a player lockout, and it didn't look like the NBA would have any season at all. Finally, in February 1999, the owners and players came to an agreement. The league decided to play a fifty-game season in eighty-five days. The battle for playoff spots would be a tough one. What was even better for the Pacers was that Jordan had retired. In fact, almost the entire Chicago Bulls team had been dismantled. There was no better time for the Pacers to get their championship.

They made it into the Eastern Conference Finals again against the Knicks, allowing Bird and his players Reggie Miller, Mark Jackson, Rik

Bird, in his second season with the team, directs strategy courtside during a February 1999 game which pitted the Philadelphia 76ers against his Indiana Pacers.

97

Smits, Chris Mullin, and the rest a taste of victory, but it would be brief. The team couldn't rebound, play defense, or shoot. The Knicks played rough basketball and took them each night.

"Reggie Miller didn't have a very good year," Bird remembered. "I kept thinking he was going to find his rhythm, but he never really did." That poor play was carried into the playoffs against the Knicks. The Pacers fought hard and made it into Game 6, but then fell apart. Miller made only three of eighteen shots. The year that was supposed to be crowned with glory was instead tainted with failure. There was little for Bird to do but blame the team's poor play. Bird decided that to get one last chance at winning a title during his third and last year as a coach, he would have to make changes to his team's lineup.

The Final Year

After the season, Bird wrote *Bird Watching* with Jackie MacMullan, a senior writer for *Sports Illustrated*. He wrote about coaching and playing in the NBA, but he also wrote about his desire to get his team over the top— to put them in the Finals and win the championship.

"We need younger players. We're going to have to make some pretty tough decisions this summer. I said in my first season I would resign rather than see this team trade Reggie or Mark Jackson. But now I realize sometimes you have to make difficult business decisions like that, for the good of the team."

The Pacers traded Antonio Davis. Bird kept his core lineup of Miller, Jackson, and Smits. He made other small lineup changes, too. He had learned a lot in the last two seasons, especially during the playoffs. He needed to use those lessons to help him get his players to a championship win.

The Pacers made the playoffs again in 2000, but to Bird it was unfinished business. He coached his players through the playoffs and into the NBA Finals. Now they had one more hurdle. It was a big one, though. The Pacers were going up against Shaquille O'Neal and the Lakers, coached by Bird's old nemesis, Phil Jackson, who had coached the Bulls for many years.

The first two games went to the Lakers. O'Neal's strong inside control dominated Smits. Bird didn't have a weapon on his team that could match O'Neal when he was hot. He didn't give up on his team, however. He knew Reggie Miller and the boys would respond, and they did in Game 3. As a coach, Bird made the right substitutions at the right time. He got the most out of every player. At the end of the game, everyone on the court was drained of energy. At the press conference, Bird told reporters, "If we didn't win today, we were in a world of trouble. We had to win a game to get back in the series, which we did."

Game 4, like Game 3, was played in Indianapolis. The hometown crowd was rabid for another win to tie the series. Again, Bird kept with the same game plan as before: Reggie shooting, Smits picking off rebounds, and Jackson racing around the floor stealing, shooting, and rebounding. The game went into overtime. Shaquille O'Neal fouled out. Miller had a final shot to win the game. Bird stood on the sidelines and watched the play that he and his assistants agreed would give Miller an open shot. As he was watched the play unfold, his heart raced. Miller cut to the wing. The pass came to him. Miller went up into the air. Laker Robert Horry raced to get a hand in Miller's face. Too late! The ball went up high, over Horry's outstretched hand. It seemed to hang in the air forever. It came down and hit the front of the rim. The buzzer sounded and the game was over. Bird could not have asked for a better shot. Miller was open, and Bird preached that the open player must take the shot. That was never a bad play. The problem was, as he had said years before, "A bad shot is anything that doesn't go in the net."

Amazingly, Bird got his team fired up for the final game in Indianapolis. The Lakers were up 3–1 in the series. Lose now and the opposing team celebrates on your home court. At the end

of the game, the Pacers had pulled off an amazing win. They clobbered the Lakers 120–87. Now they had to go back to Los Angeles and get another win to take it to Game 7.

Game 6 found Bird doing his stuff on the bench. He could not have asked for any more effort from his players. But they were simply outgunned that night and lost the game, and the championship, four games to two.

Retirement

Bird stepped down as head of the Pacers because he felt he had done all he could for the team. He was true to his word: If he couldn't get them into a position to win a championship within three years, the team would probably never win. In Bird's three years as coach, he got his team to the conference finals twice and the NBA Finals in his last year. Not many coaches have ever been able to do such wonders for any team.

He had accomplished all he could, and now he wanted to spend his days with his family. He wanted to leave the coaching life

A jubilant Reggie Miller hugs his teammate during the NBA Finals in 2000, in which Bird and his Pacers made a valiant, but unsuccessful, effort against the Lakers.

behind, with its long hours and the agonizing over missed shots. He wanted to settle down. The fans in Indiana gave him a fond farewell.

It was time to move again. This time the Bird family moved to Naples, Florida, where the weather was always perfect and he could play golf and work with the many charity organizations with which he was already involved. Each year, he hosts a celebrity golf tournament that gives more than $1 million in donations. He is always helping with charities, but his time is limited. "If I said yes to everyone, I would be working 365 days a year, and signing basketballs for the rest of my life."

Yet he is still admired by fans because he has always played with heart and coached with the wisdom learned from nearly 1,000 games. Finally, he is once again the private man who grew up in a small Midwestern town.

glossary

assist   A pass from one player to another that leads directly to a basket.

center   Usually the tallest member on a team's starting unit; the player most responsible for plays closest to the basket, including rebounding, scoring, and shot blocking.

court   The playing space for a basketball game, measuring ninety-four feet long; also called the floor, or the hardwood.

forward   One of two players flanking the center, usually on offense. Forwards play close to the basket, and must be good shooters and rebounders. They are usually taller than guards, but shorter than centers.

foul   An illegal move or contact as witnessed by the referee.

free throw   A foul shot.

guard   One of two rear players on a team, usually shorter than the forwards and the center. Guards are responsible for advancing the ball up the court and shooting from long distance.

MVP   Most valuable player, usually awarded at the All-Star Game and the NBA Finals.

NBA   National Basketball Association, founded in 1949. The NBA currently has twenty-nine teams in the United States and Canada.

pass   A move from one player to another, which may or may not include the ball making a single bounce on the court.

post   A position near the hoop. A low post has the player usually under either corner of the backboard, looking to make rebounds. High post is towards the foul line.

rebound   To retrieve the ball as it comes from the rim or backboard, taking possession for either team.

rookie   Player in his or her first professional season.

Naismith Memorial Basketball Hall of Fame
Web site: http://www.hoophall.com
The Naismith Memorial Basketball Hall of Fame
Web site has bios of all Hall of Fame members.
You can also search through a large basketball
history catalog.

National Basketball Association
Web site: http://www.nba.com
This is the official NBA Web site, where you will
find information on all teams in the league. Look
up player stats, team trades, and the latest news.
There is also a great history section for you to
look up bios on past greats of the game.

Bird, Larry, and Jackie MacMullan. *Bird Watching*. New York: Warner, 1999.

Bird, Larry, and Bob Ryan. *Drive: The Story of My Life*. New York: Bantam/ Doubleday, 1989.

Lipofsky, Steve, and Roland Lazenby. *Bird: Portrait of a Competitor*. Kansas City, MO: Addax Publishing Group, 1998.

May, Peter. *The Big Three*. New York: Simon and Schuster, 1996.

Shaw, Mark. *Larry Legend*. Lincolnwood, IL: Masters Press, 1998.

index

ig

ch

e t

ge

r

Larry Bird

About the Author

Mark Beyer is the author of more than fifty children's and young adult books. He lives in New York City.

Photo Credits

Cover © Brian Drake/SportsChrome; pp. 4, 49, 52 © AP/Wide World Photos; p. 7 © Kevin Horan/TimePix; pp. 11, 56, 66–67, 77 © Brian Drake/SportsChrome; pp. 16, 34–35 © Hulton/ Archive by Getty Images; p. 23 © Indiana State University Archives-General Photographic Collection; pp. 39, 46 © Sporting News/Archive Photos/Hulton/Archive by Getty Images; pp. 42–43, 55, 59, 61, 63 © Bettmann/Corbis; p. 73 © Reuters/Victoria Ortega/Hulton/Archive by Getty Images; p. 80–81 © Reuters/Jim Bourg/Archive by Getty Images; p. 85 © Steve Lipofsky/TimePix; pp. 88, 95, 96 © Reuters/Brent Smith/Archive by Getty Images; p. 92 © Reuters New Media Inc./Corbis; p. 102 © AFP/Corbis.

Series Design and Layout

Geri Giordano

112